How to

a Mission Strategy

Jim Currin
Church Army Evangelist
Operations Manager North East

GROVE BOOKS LIMITED
RIDLEY HALL RD CAMBRIDGE CB3 9HU

Contents

The Cover Illustration is by Peter Ashton

First Impression November 2004
ISSN 1367-0840
ISBN 1 85174 577 7

Introduction 1

'What is your strategy for mission?' asked the Bishop. 'To do nothing except pray and wait for the guidance of the Holy Spirit,' said the minister.

This true exchange illustrates one approach to mission. It is not, however, the full picture. Prayer and planning go together in Christian ministry. As in the diary, church meetings and next Sunday's sermon, it is 'both/and'; we pray and plan together.

In everyday life we plan lots of things. Imagine, for example, that you have decided to cook a meal for some special friends. Delia Smith's cookbook might inspire with recipes and pictures, but then you stop, think and plan what you can actually achieve in the time available. You might write a list, shop and make time for the occasion, remembering the old adage: 'Proper Preparation Prevents Poor Performance.' Without some planning your special meal would be a disaster!

The mission task of the local church needs no less planning. However, my own reflection over 20 years is that church leaders often plan for other things better than they do for evangelism. Renovating a roof, for example can have a well thought out 'Project Plan' with clear targets and timetable, and an exhibition in church;. while the same church's children's work might not even have a weekly budget.

Renovating a roof may have a well thought out 'Project Plan,' while the children's work might not even have a weekly budget

The aim of this material is to give you and your congregation a framework for mission and evangelism prayer and planning under the guidance of the Holy Spirit. Recognizing from the outset that most of the fruit may be in the 'process not the product' and that the key ingredients are 'consultation' and 'continuous review,' it can be adapted for use in a single church context or a group of churches and in ecumenical partnerships.

Robin Gamble wrote, 'Strategy, that is to say a good plan of action that is likely to lead to success, is not a substitute for the Spirit, it is rather a tool of the Spirit... Similarly the Spirit is not a substitute for strategy. It is not enough simply to be filled with the Spirit and then to turn up and smile at people.' He goes on to say, 'The picture of Jesus' ministry and that of the apostolic church is that of sound strategies, careful thought and planning.'[1]

This booklet is written as a 'step-by-step guide' to the prayerful preparation of a prayer and planning conference and its follow up. It is offered as one of many ways to develop a strategy. Though presented as a step-by-step guide, the assumption throughout is that you will adapt the material to suit your own situation, just as you would a food recipe.

By applying this process previous congregations have:

- Started a youth group in a garage
- Planned a 'Celebration' mission week of carefully planned events
- Started a Mother and Toddler group
- Begun a midweek 'Children's Church' after school
- Set a target to double the size of the congregation in two years
- Established a congregation modelling 'Mission Shaped Church'[2]
- Run courses like *Alpha*[3] or *Lost for Words*[4]
- Equipped Christians to witness in the workplace and in leisure interests
- Placed an appropriate gospel leaflet on the pew for funeral visitors
- Produced an evangelistic 'Tourist Trail' of local churches
- Begun 'prayer visiting,' house-to-house visits asking for requests to be offered in a special service

as well as moving forward with necessary changes such as:

- Closing a surplus church building
- Reducing the number of church meetings
- Changing the pattern of worship
- Deciding to rebuild the church building after a fire with imaginative and mission driven designs

So how do you use this material to discover your own God-given strategy?

Using this Material

These notes are chiefly written for the local church leader and prospective 'mission enabler.' The mission enabler helps facilitate the process and leads the central prayer and planning conference as an 'outside friend.' He or she may well be an external experienced church leader, belong to a mission agency or be an itinerant evangelist.

Pray and plan who is to be involved, how and when. This is a 'bottom up' not a 'top down' process, and works well when as many people as possible feel part of the prayer, planning and follow up. You may well bring a planning group together to manage the process, but ideally it should involve the whole congregation. The central conference should involve a representative body of people to represent the church family.

The preparation stage may take up to six months before the central prayer and planning conference, and the follow up another six months afterwards. The intention is that the process and plan is reviewed regularly so that it becomes an ongoing tool used in successive years.

All the suggested material for the initial 12-month process is in the text. Additional exercises looking at mission, evangelism and strategy are also offered in the Online Resources section of the Grove web site. All the exercises are deliberately brief and intended for small group discussion, for example leadership team, eldership, church council,[5] Standing Committee, cell group, or house meeting.

Perhaps it goes without saying, but all formal decisions must be the responsibility of the church council or equivalent body which gives oversight to the congregation. A sub-group may do some of the work but it is very important that the council has real ownership of the decisions, monitors the process and follows through the findings. Failure to do so has been the chief reason why some churches have failed to benefit from previous discussions on developing a strategy for mission and evangelism.

For many churches this process is not new and much of this material may already be familiar for example from church growth exercises, mission audits, bishop's vision programmes and so on.

In addition, strategies explained in *The Healthy Churches' Handbook;*[6] *Natural Church Development;*[7] or *The Purpose Driven Church*[8] are being worked out in many places. For example, you may well already have a mission statement. This material draws on, and is complementary to, all of that work…so some strategic planning may be necessary to make sure each complements the other so that a single strategy is developed.

2 Some Issues to Consider

Why Have a Strategy for Evangelism?

In church circles, we often treat strategy with suspicion. If we make plans it feels like God is being left out of the process. Some suggest that strategy sounds manipulative or un-spiritual, with God's guidance usually being discerned more by 'natural' events than a plan of action. Some critics quote the old adage, 'If you want to make God laugh, tell him your plans'!

Can a modern management term, not found in the Bible, be used in relation to God's kingdom? It is a question that cannot be ignored. For this purpose a companion paper has been placed on the Grove website where the arguments are explored, including the 'McDonaldization of the church' debate covered in the church press. For the purpose of this booklet however, it is sufficient to note the following summary which can be used for general teaching in church throughout the process:

1   The pattern and plan of creation in seven days

2   The concept of *Missio Dei* implies a strategic plan on God's part

3   The Bible speaks of God's plan for us. for example in Jer 29.11

4   The AV version of Prov 29.18 'Where there is no vision the people perish' is often quoted as a foundation text for church growth[9]

5   Jesus in Luke 4.18–19, quoting Isaiah 61.1–2, reads like a manifesto or modern mission statement

6   Jesus calls the first disciples with different gifts and characters (Luke 5.1–11)

7   Luke 10.1–11 describes a strategic approach to mission

8   Luke 14.28 assumes strategic planning in relation to faith

9   Luke 15 describes the priority of searching for the lost

10 A strategy of concentric circles is evident in Acts 1.8 'you shall be my witnesses in Jerusalem and in all Judea and Samaria and to the ends of the earth.'[10]

11 Paul's Missionary Journeys are strategically aimed at cities[11]

12 'Jesus the same yesterday, today and forever.' Heb 13.8 reflects the themes of past, present and future, used as session titles in the prayer and planning conference that is key to this process.

In brief, in this booklet, it is assumed that:

1 God has a plan;
2 Strategic planning for mission is a God-given opportunity;
3 Prayerful planning makes our ministry both more efficient and more effective.

A Comment on Personality

Some people have problems with the concept of planning and God's purpose. All kinds of reasons might contribute to this—personality, upbringing, work experience, role in a group. Most often, however, it has been found that 'brain dominance' has been the key factor, so a comment is offered here.

Each of us has a dominant side of the brain which affects the way we think. 'Left brain dominant' people tend to be logical, tidy and like things organized, while the 'right brain dominant' tend to be more creative and spontaneous. Strategists tend to be 'left brain linear' people and find this process straight forward, whereas the 'right brain creative' people sometimes find it difficult. Both personality types have much to contribute and this material and process values both, especially in the discussion exercises.

Companion Books

Companion books well worth having along side this material are:

1 *The Healthy Churches' Handbook* by Robert Warren, as he explores the 'Seven Marks' of healthy churches from research and experience in many different settings.[12]
2 *Evangelism—Which Way Now?* by Mike Booker and Mark Ireland as they evaluate various strategies like *Alpha, Emmaus,* cell church and Natural Church Development.[13]
3 *Developing Visionary Leadership* by Williams and Tanner in the Grove Renewal series. They emphasize the leader building teams and working for SMART targets.[14]
4 *Mission-Shaped Church* by Paul Bayes.[15] The previous Grove booklet in the Evangelism series looked at the Anglican report of the same title, with an emphasis on values which underline mission, so we do not just get on the latest bandwagon.

Some Working Definitions

Mission or 'God's sending activity' has been described as

> ...the creating, reconciling and transforming action of God, flowing from the community of love in the Trinity, made known to all humankind in the person of Jesus, and entrusted to the faithful action and witness of the people of God, who, in the power of the Spirit, are a sign, foretaste and instrument of the reign of God.[16]

This is a broad description of everything God sends us out to do.

Evangelism is much more specific. It is the first of the 'Five Marks of Mission' to 'Proclaim the Good news of the Kingdom';[17] although, as David Jeans points out, 'defining evangelism is not quite as simple, and there is overlap with some of the other Marks.'[18]

Bosch provides a good summary definition:

> To make known by word and deed the love of the crucified and risen Christ in the power of the Holy Spirit, so that people will repent, believe and receive Christ as their saviour and obediently serve him as their Lord in the fellowship of the church.[19]

This booklet assumes that evangelism is about 'sharing the gospel' and 'making disciples' of Jesus, in relation both to the individual and to the church. We shall think of how the church provides a platform as the means and medium for the gospel.[20]

'Developing a strategy' here means thinking of who does what, how and when in mission and evangelism, with appropriate planning and follow up. It can include the detail of church notice boards and appropriate gospel literature in the pew for visitors. It is a process that looks first at purpose, then plans and then projects, so that the church is more efficient and effective in fulfilling the evangelistic task.

'Developing a strategy here means thinking of who does what, how and when in mission and evangelism

> Developing a strategy for mission and evangelism is simply about putting thought, prayer, order and planning into the God-given task.

The 'God of Surprises' and Changing Plans

Writing about planning strategies for evangelism, Booker and Ireland strikingly say in their Preface:

> In our experience our most fruitful evangelistic encounters have not come through carefully planned strategies, but through responding to unexpected opportunities that God has placed in front of us...a strategy for evangelism is really useful, both in creating the climate of possibility and in equipping people to make the most of the opportunities, but perhaps the most important thing churches need to do is to be prayerful—so that they recognize God's surprising opportunities when they come.[21]

The guidance of the Spirit was often a surprise, as in Acts where Philip was directed to go up a desert road, and then forbidden to go to the towns and villages (Acts 8.26–40).

In the same way as the good Samaritan had to change his plans for the day in responding to the need of the Levite, we might have to change our plans in response to given circumstances (Luke 10.25–37).

God may change our plans, or we may have difficulties as:

a some people naturally find the process 'awkward';
b sometimes we just cannot discern God's will;
c life can be too complex to plan strategically.

Interestingly, Rick Warren in *The Purpose Driven Church* writes about one of his favourite movies, *Raiders of the Lost Ark*. At one point Jones is hanging on by his finger tips over a snake pit when someone asks, 'What are you going to do now?' to which Jones replies, 'How do I know? I'm making it up as we go along!' For someone writing a major work on being 'purpose driven' it is significant that Warren says, 'I have felt like that many, many times.'[22]

The 'yes, but' caveat to strategic planning is important to acknowledge in prayer and discussion throughout the process.

3

Step 1: The Preparation

The Preparation stage could take six months.

The purpose is to prepare for a prayer and planning conference. This is a sensible amount of time if a lot of groups are involved in thinking about mission, evangelism and strategy, especially if they produce a mission statement.

It is important to go at the right speed so that everyone in the church feels the process has open access. As they say: 'To be real it has to be local; to be effective it has to be practical'; to which we might add, 'to be owned it has to be "everyone."'

At this point it is also important to recognize that strategy is only part of the picture. Allan Landall suggested that church growth requires vision, leadership and strategy just as fire requires oxygen, heat and fuel to burn.[23] Removing any one of these critical elements will put the spiritual fire out.

The Venn diagram on the right can be shown as a series of overhead projector or Powerpoint slides: the final one being simply 'Jesus.' This is a reminder that he is the focus of all that we are seeking to do. This diagram could relate to managing a business, but in mission and evangelism we 'keep our eyes fixed on Jesus' (Mt 14.28–32).

So the emerging strategy will also require emerging vision and leadership. The vision needs to be corporately owned by the congregation and the leadership carefully exercised—not telling people what to do, but enabling them to come to common, agreed conclusions with motivation and enthusiasm. The following exercises, appropriately used, can help in that task.

Exercise 1: 'What Are We Trying To Do?'

This exercise is for a planning group which may have been appointed to see through the whole process. The aim is to try to agree a local working definition of evangelism to both give the congregation something to use and quote, and to shape the emerging strategy.

Use lists of various Bible and general quotations to get the group started. See for example the CPAS 'Creating Confidence in Evangelism' list.[24]

Brainstorm the common key words from the list and write them up on a flipchart. Use them to pull together the key concepts of evangelism and invite the group to write their own simple single definition of evangelism which is memorable, in no more than say 10–15 words. This can become a working definition and guide which can be quoted frequently. If a single definition is not forthcoming, agree the core elements and quote them as a tick list.

Exercise 2: The Haggai Question: 'Consider How You Have Fared'

This exercise can be used in a variety of different groups and settings. The aim is to ask each group to consider how well it does evangelism.

Use the agreed definition of evangelism from the exercise above and ask the Haggai Question (see Haggai 1.1–11): 'How well are we doing our evangelism?' or, to put it sharply, 'How are we making disciples?' Collate the conclusions in the planning group. Report back in a sermon and magazine article what have been the general findings and common perception. It is even useful to adapt the question for community groups or individuals to see how effective they perceive the outreach of the church to be.

Exercise 3: Lessons From the World of Work

This is best considered by the planning group. The aim is to draw on the experience of people in the congregation.

Interestingly, secular bodies frequently use words like purpose, vision, values and particularly mission statements, when the church is hesitant to utilize them.

Many people in management roles or on governing bodies will be familiar with principles of strategic management where purpose, priorities and plans need to decided and reviewed on a regular basis.

Perhaps you have a member of the congregation who is working with these concepts all the time at work. Invite them to speak about the processes from that work context. Suggest they develop such themes as 'mentoring,' 'life coaching' and 'learning organizations' in relation to Christian discipleship; or 'fit for purpose' in relation to church building and structure, or 'process management' in relation to developing a strategy for evangelism.

Exercise 4: Care Plan for a Healthy Church

This exercise is for the planning group, eldership team, or house groups. The aim is to consider 1 Corinthians 12.12–26 as Bible study material. Here the writer uses the human body as a metaphor for the church. So, how healthy is it? How can it be fully fit?

Health professionals use a Care Plan for each patient. The Plan is based on a review process, which involves the key stages of assessment, planning, implementation and evaluation.

Ask the group to consider these headings with the questions for the church:

> 1 What is your assessment of the 'patient' at present?
> 2 What are the signs of sickness and health?
> 3 What is need to improve the health of the church?
> 4 How can we plan to make these improvements?
> 5 How might you implement the plan? By when?
> 6 What resources are needed?
> 7 How can the progress be reviewed and evaluated?

Think through how the congregation can consider the suggested plan and pray individually, in groups, for the way forward as a body.

Exercise 5: Benchmarks

This is an exercise for the leadership team or planning group. The aim is to use comparison as a technique for planning.

The benchmark is an old practice of the carpenter. It is a way of comparing something being done with an accurate measurement. The following are models of mission practice which we can use as benchmarks for the local church.

For example, type up the 'Five Marks of Mission' on OHP acetate and use this benchmark as a discussion starter for the planning group. See any strengths as things to be celebrated and weaknesses as areas to be addressed.

You will need to be very discerning about this exercise and only choose one model at a time. This exercise can soon lead to 'information overload' so do not go in to it in great depth, unless you use, for example, the full *Natural Church Development* or *Healthy Churches* material as a full follow up.

- Five Marks of Mission[25]
- Eight quality signs of Natural Church Development[26]
- Seven aspects of growing Healthy Churches[27]
- Millennium Welcome Challenge[28]

Preparing a Mission Statement

If you already have a mission statement, revisit the process by which it came to be written. Ask whether it is owned by all members of the congregation, and whether it is often quoted or used, apart from on notice boards and letterheads where it is a permanent feature. Does it shape the work of the church on a day to day basis? Is yours a Mission, Vision, or Purpose Statement? Is your aim clear to those who read it?

If you do not have a Statement, it is worthwhile devising one at this point. The mission enabler could help the congregation do this. You may compose it in the Prayer and Planning conference which follows, but if it is done now in the Preparation stage more people can be involved and it may lead to greater ownership later on.

The place to start is to take Billy Graham's advice about the three most important aspects of planning evangelism, 'The first is prayer. The second is prayer. And the third…is prayer.' Begin the activity with prayer and an appropriate Bible reflection, for example Luke 4.18–19.

> A mission statement is not just a collective view of what we think we should be doing as a church; it is God's purpose we are seeking to discern for our work in extending his kingdom.

Of all the various ways of putting a mission statement together the easiest and most effective has been to ask individuals to complete the sentence, 'The aim of our church is…' The challenge is to complete the sentence in no more than 25 words, within a given time.

Everyone could do this, using a slip of paper, from children to the oldest member. One church put slips in a box on local shop counters and invited people from the community to contribute too, but that may not be appropriate where you are.

If a lot of people have done this, the planning group needs to collate the contributions and propose a new single sentence. This proposal then needs to be discussed and ratified in the church council, for reporting back throughout the congregation. If the exercise is to be kept for the conference, see the relevant notes in the next section.

4

Step 2: The Prayer and Planning Conference

The focal point of this process is the conference.

It can be a day or preferably a weekend away. Time away from the church setting provides precious space for prayer and a creative planning process which is unobtainable in the normal busyness of life.

To be most effective, the conference needs to be planned as if it were a retreat with activities. The planning group could introduce each session with worship, readings and prayer. The overall biblical theme of past, present and future, using Heb 13.8 is useful.

The main activity sessions are led by the mission enabler. He or she is not only invaluable, but almost essential. This person can ask the naïve questions and help the group work well. It is highly desirable that the leader is neutral and outside the usual politics and personalities in a way that the congregation leader is not.

At a relevant point suggest that conference rules of active listening, acceptance of different views and confidentiality be kept.

The Programme

An article in the *Church Times* suggested that the chief mark of a successful church was not so much large numbers and plenty of activity, but play.[29] The time away may be a rare opportunity for people to get together and enjoy fun, food, and fellowship. The actual programme for the conference needs to reflect the importance of this as well as the tasks that they are going to try to achieve.

A fun introduction is to suggest that everyone says their name, any church responsibility and something unusual about themselves that no-one else might know. All this information is needed for the weekend leader—but is also helpful and interesting for everyone else!

Conference Session 1: The Past—How Did We Get Here?
After worship and some 'getting to know you' exercises, the first main session provides an opportunity to look back as a church.[30]

1   A good introduction, especially if you are the mission enabler and new to the group, is to ask for recommendations of somewhere in the parish that provides a good lunch.

'Oh there's nowhere close to us, you've got to go a few miles if you want a really nice pub lunch' might be one reply. Ask why the recommendations are highly rated and list the attributes on a flipchart. Usually it is to do with atmosphere, easy access, being comfortable, efficient service delivery and, of course, good food. People begin to catch on to the fact this question is really a way of getting people to talk about 'what makes for a good church.'

2   A more direct starting point is to ask: 'How did you start coming to church?' or simply 'Why do you go to church?' or 'Tell me why your church is worth joining.'[31] The answers are often quite revealing. Always emphasize the positive points. List them on a flipchart. Think how this list might determine a strategy for mission in the future, on the basis that if the church has attracted you for certain reasons, it might attract others into the fellowship. Though theologically not ideal, like tends to attract like.[32]

3   It might be possible to discuss 'How the gospel came to us.' A short consideration of church history might be relevant. Certainly trying to get a picture of how the first Christians were converted can help some people think of how this could happen today. Someone will need to have prepared this information in the preparation stage for presentation in the conference.

Reference to the 1851 Census can be a revelation to correct stereotypical views of church-going in the past. It may be possible to get a copy of the 1851 Ward return of relevant local church attendance. Contrary to popular opinion, it can be seen that not everyone went to church. It was 1 in 4 in many areas and often no higher than 1 in 3 even in urban areas.

4   Ask the question about what has happened to the people who used to attend church as children. What has happened to them? *Gone but not Forgotten*[33] and *A Churchless Faith*[34] are further resource books for those particularly interested in this question. Sometimes groups need pushing to see that many people have left the church, raising the question about the nature of church in the eyes of people who do not attend.

Further detail can be found in church registers. Arrange beforehand for someone to draw a graph of attendance over the past ten years in preparation for this session. Suggest that groups do not talk about personalities but the trends and principles of church membership.

5   The chief exercise for this first Conference Session is the timeline for the past ten years. If you have sufficient numbers, split into three groups with a minimum of four people in each group. If you have representatives of several churches, for instance from a rural group, suggest that each group represents its own church. Note that some people will not know the history over ten years so they might need to do a shorter line.

Begin by asking the groups to think of the major 'church' events that have occurred over the past ten years. When did they occur? Were they significantly good in building the life of the congregation or were they disasters? Note that a church fire can be both good and bad! Each group should list the events and discuss significance on flipchart paper.

Then, having listed the events they remember, each group is given an OHP acetate marked out like this:

-10	-9	-8	-7	-6	-5	-4	-3	-2	-1	This Year

Suggest the major events are noted on the timescale to show when they occurred (three years ago = -3 and so on) as a mark on the sheet. Ask each group to suggest whether they were a positive (above the line) or negative (below) influence on the congregation, and by how much.

It might be difficult, but if it is possible suggest a line be drawn through the events. This timeline illustrates the perceived ups and downs of the church over the past ten years.

The conclusions from each of the groups can be reported back and compared with each other by overlaying the OHPs. Accept all views offered and draw out general conclusions. The most interesting part of this exercise is to see if agreement is reached. In particular, see if the far right of the graph is going up or down, as this illustrates how people perceive the church now.

This timeline illustrates the perceived ups and downs of the church over the past ten years

16

6   A good alternative exercise for this session can be found in *Change Directions* by David Cormack[35] when he suggests people draw three circles to represent the past, the present and the future life of the church. Ten ways of drawing the circles in relation to each other are detailed in the book. Group suggestions can be discussed in relation to Cormack's list. Just like the time-line it reveals people's perceptions which need to feed in to the prayer and planning.

Conference Session 2: The Present: Where Are We Going?
If you have omitted Session 1, you will need to start with some devotional introduction and a warm up exercise, before proceeding to the following teaching on the four dimensions of growth.

Assuming this is Session 2, begin with some prayer and reflection on the 'time lines' produced by the three groups. Did the end of each line look as if the church was on the up? Celebrate it if that is the case and all the groups agree. If not, suggest a time of prayer seeking God to arrest the decline. Finally, consider the points of growth on each line. These may be indicators of possible future growth, which can be in one of Four Dimensions:[36]

Four Dimensions of Growth

1   Upwards—in greater knowledge of God (Heb 5.11–6.3)

2   Together—into greater fellowship (Rom 12.1–13)

3   Outwards—in service to other people, and (Luke 4.16–21; 7.18–23)

4   More—in numbers attending worship (Mark 4.1–20)

This list can be abbreviated to: Up, Together, Out and More.

You might do a presentation about growth and evangelism, suggesting that 1,2 and 3 are often the pre-requisite of 4. This is an important aspect of teaching which needs to be grasped by the conference.

As this process is about evangelism, it may be appropriate to take the opportunity to help conference members think about their own relationship with God. To demonstrate the first dimension of growth (Up), show an OHP slide or Powerpoint presentation of the Engel Scale.[37] After a brief explanation ask people to reflect on where they are themselves on the scale. Prayer and a time for personal commitment might well follow, before proceeding.

Next, it can be useful splitting the conference into the three groups again to discuss the other three dimensions of growth. These discussions will also pick up on the 'concentric circles' of Acts 1.8.

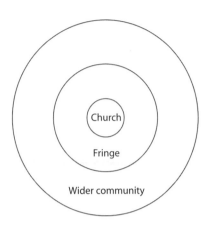

*'You shall be my witnesses in Jerusalem, and in all Judea and Samaria, and to the ends of the earth'... **or** in the church, fringe and wider community...*

Group 1 can think of the inner circle of the church fellowship. They brainstorm a list, or draw a 'spider diagram' of all the church activities and groups in the congregation. Then they suggest ways in which these groups can encourage growth 'Up, Together, Out or More.' Examples could be: introducing Bible notes; thinking through a welcome ministry[38]; planning a joint children's and old people's party; or a memorial service with healing ministry. It can be a long list for further consideration.

Group 2 think of the fringe. Is this group getting smaller or larger in your church? You might discuss who are the 'de-churched' who once belonged, or those who attend church less than once a month. List the organizations and groups which have some link with the church and discuss 'Up, Together, Out and More.' Highlight particular people or possible projects that can reach out and draw in. John Clarke suggests many people join our church by 'osmosis'[39] so how can this process be encouraged?

Group 3 list the groups in the wider local community, and church people who are involved in them. Suggest how links can be strengthened and bridges built with community projects. Consider how the gospel message is heard in the groups you already have links with. *Building Bridges of Hope*[40] is a resource regarding this and can be used in the Follow Up stage. *Mission-Shaped Church* is now seminal reading, so how can you establish church for the un-churched in your own local community?

Alternatively, this group might draw a simple map of the area around the church building(s), marking where members of the congregation live and what physical factors might influence the mission strategy (for better or worse). List where people naturally congregate (pubs, leisure centres, bus shelters and car boot sales) and ask the question, 'Where would Jesus be?' Is this an indication of where you might create church for the unchurched?

Each group may well have a long list of proposals for prayer and consideration in the next session. Before moving on, however, the conference should consider:

1 The Acts 1.8 picture of concentric circles looks static whereas mission implies movement. The mission of the church (sending out) should be seen as a spiritual 'centrifugal force,' while the response of people who are drawn in is a 'centripetal force.'

2 Many people are right outside the reach of the church, so the starting point might be to 'stop starting with the church.' The conference should be reminded of the un-churched and de-churched people that *Mission-Shaped Church* addresses.

3 The proposals made will be many and varied. All will go to the planning group but only some can surface onto what shall become a mission action plan. It is to be anticipated that after all the teaching, prayer and preparation, the chosen projects will provide a focus for future mission and evangelism.

Each group now needs to share their conclusions with the full conference. Lists on acetate sheets make reporting back easier and provide a ready record for future reference. Now it is time to move on to the next session — prayerful planning for the future.

Conference Session 3: The Future: How are we going to get there?
The chief tools in this whole process are the mission statement (MS) and mission action plan (MAP). They can now be put together. If you already have them,[41] they can be considered afresh with the new material from conference Session 2. Begin the session with prayer for God's guidance as you propose your strategy together. As an introduction, reflect on the ministry of Jesus and the purpose of the church. You might ask people to list 'kingdom activities' and compare them with the 'church activities.' This is in preparation for asking the question, 'What **ought** the church to be doing in mission?' rather than 'What **is** the church doing?' Introduce the MS concept if it is new.

Your Mission Statement (MS)

If you already have inherited or recently written one, can everyone quote it? How is it used? Does it make a difference? Rick Warren in *The Purpose Driven Church*[42] suggests that the congregation is taught from it once a month. Do you refer to it that often?

Consider your MS and review it in the light of the emerging themes of the conference. If you did not compose it in the preparation stage, do so now.

Say that this is a listening exercise—listening both to God and to each other. Ask people to reflect and write their 'The aim of this church is…' sentence in a set period of silence, say three minutes. Then suggest people compare notes in pairs, and being generous to each others suggestions, write a new joint MS sentence of 25 words between them. This process is repeated until you get a conference conclusion on to a flipchart. It is sometimes hard work but always well worth it!

Suggest this MS is a working definition of what the church is aiming at for now. Recognize differences of opinion and say that they will be considered by the relevant church authority, along with the MAP, as they finally ratify the conclusions.

Mission Action Plan (MAP)

Refer back to the time of prayer and the lists of suggestions proposed in Session 2 by the three groups. Suggest that the MS should shape the proposals now to be made on the MAP.

So, suggest that individually and prayerfully, everyone reflects on all the discussion so far. Ask each person to jot down on paper what they think God wants the church to do, in line with the MS. The proposals should be:

1 On a list of no more than ten suggestions per person
2 Each reflecting one of the four dimensions of growth
3 Focussed on mission and evangelism
4 Preferably in priority order
5 SMART[43] (specific, measurable, achievable,[44] realistic and time bound)

Now, get the groups to meet again and direct them to each draw up a single list of ten suggestions. These will become proposals. Recognize that some will be easy to fulfil (a very SMART target would be someone offering to provide coffee after church on the following Sunday) while others will need major project planning—a building project or new congregation. These factors will all be absorbed in the MAP.

The groups come together and compare the lists. Overlaps are noted and a single conference list agreed, on flipchart, OHP or Powerpoint. Note that all suggestions can be considered by the planning group or church leadership, so nothing is lost. However, the group need to make the list manageable (SMART targets again). This new list is to form the start of the MAP. Try to arrange the 1–10 list in priority order, suggesting that each proposal is to become an 'action in mission' (AIM for short).

This is an apt time to suggest the conference avoids 'initiative overload.' It may be wise to revise the list to make it balanced and manageable. You might spend some time thinking about the current church activities which could cease in order to make way for the new AIMs. In particular the mission enabler needs to ask about the purpose in mission behind each AIM, and how more specific evangelism will result.

Before the final list of ten AIMs is agreed, the enabler leader should remind the group of the fundamental purpose of developing a strategy for evangelism. If agreed, weight can be given to proposals which are clearly more mission than maintenance.

If all has gone well you should be able to produce a summary report, as below, showing of the general conclusions with the MS and MAP with AIMs in the first column.

When filling in the MAP below, it is worth remembering Kipling's quote: *'I keep six honest serving-men (They taught me all I knew); Their names are What and Why and When And How and Where and Who.'*[45]

The main aim of our church is to ....(=MS)..........which will mean we aim to:

Our AIMs	For growth Up, Together, Out or More	For whom	By whom	By when	NOTE
1					
2					
3					
4					
5					

and so on up to a maximum of ten rows.

This is the point at which you, as the outside mission enabler, might ask some difficult questions. For example:

1 Are all our church activities aimed at one of the four dimensions of growth?
2 Does all current church activity meet the criteria for what we ought to be doing, as described in the MS?

3 If not, what should be the course of action?
4 Are any aspects of church life wasteful, inefficient, unhelpful or unnecessary to the ministry and mission of the congregation?
5 Are some of the things we do a distraction to our main purpose of worship and making disciples of Jesus?

It is important that the conference does not get too distracted with detail, especially in these difficult questions, as the MS and MAP is coming together. Take the group as far as they have the energy to go. You may have to simply flag up some suggestions for the church leadership or council to consider.

After the conference, the planning group can collate all the material and work on it further before presenting it for discussion, decision and implementation. If your conference has been able to produce an agreed MS and MAP it has worked hard. Members should be thanked, and asked to continue praying for the process as it continues in the follow up stage.

5

Step 3: The Follow Up

On returning from the conference, the planning group may have to meet to collate and prepare a presentation of all the findings so far.

In particular they may work on the details of the MS and MAP ready for the next regular church council or equivalent. This presentation must happen, even if all the members were at the conference! This is because conclusions from a weekend away need to be ratified in the cold light of day by the due authority of the church. The MS and MAP can and should be owned from then on.

When agreeing the MS and further details of the MAP, encourage the council to work on it further, being prayerful, generous and strategic in their thinking too. Emphasize again the need for the focus to be on mission and evangelism, with SMART targets, and with implications considered.

The MS and MAP should now be presented to the congregation. This also needs thinking through strategically in order that everyone understands and owns the conclusions drawn. As in the preparation stage, it is important that all groups and individuals in the congregation feel that this is a process with open access. Implications can then be explored with those affected by decisions made in the church council.

In presenting your MS and MAP to the congregation you might describe them as purpose, plans, priorities and projects.

Reports and presentations should lead to further discussion, reflection and more exercises throughout the congregation, listed as Exercises 6–10 below. The important thing is that you keep the momentum going through sermons, magazine articles, discussion, display material and so on, so that everyone owns the priorities and new projects. The mission enabler may be able to help with this ongoing process. Modern IT presentations make it possible to present information in an eye-catching and interesting way.

> *The MS* should become a fairly permanent fixture in the congregation life. It needs to be memorable, owned, and frequently used.
>
> *The MAP*, on the other hand, needs to have a shorter shelf life and be fairly flexible. It is simply a proposed plan and needs an annual review of its implementation.

Be very clear about the criteria for change, especially if it is to do with sensitive areas, so that people are not distracted with detail and lose sight of the overall aim and strategic thinking which has led to the conclusion. The key thing is to celebrate practical outcomes of the process and consider how the gospel message can shared through them.

The extent to which the MAP can be developed and used will depend on local circumstances. A smaller church may just identify three priorities for the coming year. Others will resemble a full business plan with priorities, projects, names, timescale and review procedure all written down. Either way it needs to be of most use, and appropriate for your context.

For significant AIM proposals a member of the planning team might work with a particular group to produce a specific project plan.

When feeding back the MS and MAP to the wider congregation and groups within it, refer to 'Some Issues to Consider' as they are bound to come up, but try not to let them be a distraction. Refer people to the accompanying Grove website paper on strategy if they wish to explore theology and praxis.

As in the preparation stage, carefully plan the communication strategy and incorporate the different ways people think, and personality types, into the process. Listen to the comments and observations made. Always emphasize prayer, as the AIM projects are to be implemented over the coming weeks and months.

Explain that the process, the plan, and each AIM project are not fixed, but open to continuous review. The simplest, and most memorable, review cycle can be called the ADA principle, depicted here in diagram form.

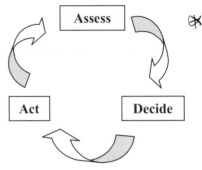

Although you made an *assessment* in the preparation stage, *decided* in the conference and now *act* in the implementation follow up, keep in mind the continuous nature of the ADA principle. You continue to assess what people act on and go round the cycle again. The most obvious way this happens is with an annual review at the church AGM, which may well suggest a follow up conference the following year to review the MAP and move forward again.

As people work through the AIMs, make it clear how long the MAP is intended to be used for, and when each AIM will be reviewed. The planning group might monitor the progress of each AIM and plan an interim day of prayer for the progress. As part of that day, or in other suitable meetings or groups, you might usefully employ these further exercises, which follow on from Exercises 1 to 5 used in the preparation stage. They can be used with a wide variety of groups and in different situations as the process continues.

Exercise 6: The People I Meet in a Week

This is similar to an exercise developed by CPAS in their six-week *Lost for Words* course.[46] The exercise can be for house groups or in a sermon slot. The aim is to help Christians consider their own personal 'mission field.'

Give everyone a pencil and piece of paper with the picture of the sun from Microsoft Word 'AutoShapes.'

Ask them, in two minutes, to draw their own portrait in the centre. After lots of laughter and embarrassment, suggest the serious point of the exercise about the people we meet in a week and the way we might shine for Jesus.

Suggest that the sun's rays point to groups — church, work, family, hobby — or individuals. Make it clear that we all have different networks. As the conference leader you might display your own offering, suggesting that the picture becomes a picture for prayer of our own individual mission field.

Exercise 7: Who are the Evangelists Among You?

This is for the planning group or church council. The aim is to discern who might be released from other church responsibilities for evangelism.

Ephesians 4 assumes that there are evangelists in the body of Christ. So who are they? Do they know they have that ministry? How do they develop it?

Evangelists come forward in many ways. Some have a particular gift of inviting others to Christian events. Others can be described as having a ministry of welcome, or naturally speak of Jesus over coffee, while others have gifts in more formal settings, like preaching and teaching. Discerning those who are good at running an *Alpha* course group, or who might give a testimony in a coffee morning, requires some thought, prayer, and planning. It can require some people being released from other responsibilities in order to exercise their God-given role.

Spend some useful time thinking about the people in the congregation and what they do, both at church and outside it. Think of hobbies as well as work and community networks they might have. How can these people be encouraged in their evangelistic task? Try to get an overview of everyone. Pray about any role changes, training, coaching, recognition, or just general encouragement these people might need to fulfil their mission potential.

Encourage further thought. For example, when suggesting names of people alongside particular AIMs, think what they might stop doing to make space for it. Try to have people exercise a ministry God would want them to have, utilising their talents and personalities to best advantage.

Exercise 8: SWOT Analysis

This is for any leader. The aim of this well-known exercise is to analyse any activity or proposal.

You list the relative strengths, weaknesses, opportunities and threats (= SWOT) of the chosen activity. As an example, think of the church which bought a local hotel which become vacant opposite. A SWOT list could be:

Strengths — a focus on mission; an imaginative project
Weaknesses — perhaps the strain on leaders and church structure
Opportunity — having an unthreatening venue for the unchurched
Threats — the cost of conversion and complaints from neighbours

Think of your own activities and AIMs on the MAP and do a SWOT analysis.

Exercise 9: Double or Quit?

This question could be for any group and the congregation as a whole. If the church is very small indeed, ask individuals. The aim is to offer a challenge.

Ask this question: 'If we were going to double the size of this congregation in the next 12 months, how would we go about it?' You might add: 'and make your suggestions SMART, that is, specific, measurable, achievable, realistic and time bound.'

Report back in a sermon or magazine article with the list of all the suggestions made.

Exercise 10: Our Own 'Performance Targets'

This is another exercise which any group could consider, but it can be threatening for some. The aim is to consider our own 'performance targets.'

We have become familiar with performance targets. Whether it be trains running to time, amount of rubbish cleared or hospital waiting lists being reduced, we live in a culture where public organizations are accountable to their customers.

Now this is a fun exercise! You will be asking the group to think of the performance targets we might have in church.

To a certain extent we do this when keeping a record of attendance. But how often do we set out to think of 'targets'? Perhaps the only time we do this is when raising money and we have a certain figure to find. This can be an incentive and help everyone feel that something is achieved when reached.

So, using the principle of targets, discuss some mission activities, which are measurable. Doubling the congregation might be one, or one person bringing one more per year could be another. Discuss 'success' and 'failure' in this context and the '7 out of 10' principle of what might be reasonably achieved. Rarely do we achieve 10/10 of what we set out to do, and 4/10 would be poor performance. As a church leader rate your own performance targets as an individual and as a church in ministry and mission.

Conclusion 6

There is much scope for further work to be done with such concepts as 'risk and reward' theory or 'reactive and proactive' planning.

Indeed, forthcoming Grove booklets might consider project planning, creating 'mission-shaped church' initiatives, planning with the un-churched, or even 'intuitive evangelism'!

However, this adaptable material has focussed on developing a strategic plan for mission and evangelism through the local church. Using simple tools of a MS, MAP and AIMs the local body of Christ has been encouraged to discern God's plan for mission, making best use of their own resources.

This is not about telling God what to do. Proverbs 19.21 reminds us that 'the human mind may devise many plans, but it is the purpose of the Lord that will be established.' The hope is that what has been discerned is not a sticking plaster strategy, but a well thought out, positive plan which helps the church move out in mission and evangelism with some 'centrifugal' force into the wider community.

We should continue to pray for God's guidance in that ongoing task of making 'his last command our first concern.'[47]

Notes

1   Robin Gamble, *The Irrelevant Church* (Monarch, 1992) p 155.
2   *Mission-Shaped Church* (Church House Publishing, 2004).
3   www.alphacourse.org
4   *Lost for Words*: A six-session course from CPAS, Athena Drive, Tachbrook Park, Warwick. CV34 6NG (01926 458458). Companion book: James Lawrence, *Lost for Words* (BRF, 1999).
5   'Church council' will be used as a generic term for whatever group is responsible for authority in your church.
6   Robert Warren, *The Healthy Churches' Handbook* (CHP, 2004).
7   Christian Schwartz, *Natural Church Development* (BCGA, 1996).
8   Rick Warren, *The Purpose Driven Church* (Zondervan, 1995).
9   See for example Peter Brierley in *Vision Building* (Hodder and Stoughton, 1989) p 15.
10 Explored for example by Steve Legg in *A-Z of Evangelism* (Hodder and Stoughton, 2002) p 185.
11 *cf* Donald Senior and Carroll Stuhlmueller, *The Biblical Foundations for Mission* (SCM, 1983) p 141 and p 182, and Robin Gill and Derek Burke, *Strategic Church Leadership* (SPCK, 1996) p 10.
12 Robert Warren, *The Healthy Churches' Handbook* (CHP, 2004).
13 Mike Booker and Mark Ireland, *Evangelism—Which Way Now?* (CHP, 2003).
14 Richard Williams and Mark Tanner, *Developing Visionary Leadership* (Grove Renewal booklet, R 17).
15 Paul Bayes, *Mission-Shaped Church* (Grove Evangelism booklet, Ev 67).
16 MISSIO, *Anglicans in Mission: A Transforming Journey* (SPCK, 2000) p 21.
17 *ibid*, p 20.
18 *Inside Out: The Report of the Church Army's Theology of Evangelism Working Party 2004* (Church Army/ SPCK) p 46.
19 David Bosch, *Transforming Mission* (Orbis, 1991) p 420.
20 'Church' in the context of this booklet usually refers to what Robert Warren and the recent report *Mission-Shaped Church*, might describe as 'inherited' rather than 'emerging' mode.
21 Booker and Ireland, *op cit*, p xii.
22 Rick Warren, *Purpose Driven Church* (Zondervan, 1995) p 28.
23 Allan R Landall, *Your Church Can Grow* (Leicester Diocesan Evangelism Committee, 1995) p 9.
24 John Young, *Creating Confidence in Evangelism* (CPAS, 1991) p 13.
25 MISSIO, *op cit*, p 20.
26 *Natural Church Development*, *op cit*, p 79.
27 *The Healthy Churches' Handbook*, *op cit*, p 110.
28 Listed in A Gilchrist, Grove Evangelism booklet Ev 66 *Creating a Culture of Welcome in the Local Church*
29 The Revd Dr Adrian Hough, *Church Times*, 1st Aug 2003.
30 This is the least necessary session and can be left out if only a handful of people can be gathered for a short day away together.
31 Jack Nichols and Cyril Ashton wrote on this theme in *A Faith Worth Sharing? A Church Worth Joining?* (DLT, 1995).
32 In missiological study it is often called the 'Homogenous Unit Principle' after Donald McGavran in *Understanding Church Growth* (Grand Rapids, 1970) p 223 said that 'men like to become Christians without crossing racial, linguistic or class barriers.' The 'Homogenous Unit Principle' is to still be debated. See papers in an internet search from *Google* for further consideration.
33 Philip Richter and Leslie J Francis, *Gone but not Forgotten* (DLT, 1998).
34 Alan Jamieson, *A Churchless Faith* (SPCK, 2002).
35 David Cormack, *Change Directions* (Monarch, 1995) p 46ff.
36 From *Is My Church Worth Joining?* a workbook prepared for Mission England by the Bible Society, 1984.
37 Considered by Laurence Singlehurst, *Sowing Reaping Keeping* (Crossway, 1998) p 18ff.
38 See Alison Gilchrist, Grove Evangelism booklet Ev 66 *Creating a Culture of Welcome in the Local Church*
39 John Clarke, *Evangelism That Really Works* (SPCK, 1995) pp 19–20.
40 www.ctbi.org.uk/bbh or www.ccom.org.uk
41 Some regional church leaders *eg* diocesan Bishops have asked every church to produce them, or you may have produced the MS in the preparation stage.
42 Rick Warren, *op cit*, p 117.
43 *cf Developing Strategic Leadership, op cit*, p 10.
44 Sometimes references suggest 'A' is 'Agreed.'
45 Rudyard Kipling, 'I keep six honest serving-men': *Oxford Dictionary of Quotations* (OUP, 1989) p 300.
46 For details contact CPAS, Athena Drive, Tachbrook Park, Warwick CV34 6NG, www.cpas.org.uk
47 Phrase used by *Evangelism Explosion*: www.ee-gb.org.uk